Thirty-Three Ways to Help with Reading

Thirty-Three Ways to Help with . . .

Series Editor: Linda Evans

This series of practical 'how-to' books is for teachers, teaching assistants and SENCOs who are in need of fresh ideas to teach pupils in their care who are struggling with basic skills. Each title provides tools enabling practitioners to make good provision for a range of children in their class. Practical ideas and materials can be extracted without needing to plough through chapters of theory and research.

All titles are A4 in format, photocopiable, and include an introduction and clearly presented activity pages.

Written by experienced practitioners and experts, this series is a lifeline to anyone facing the challenge of teaching children who are struggling.

Titles in the series so far:

Thirty-Three Ways to Help with Numeracy by Brian Sharp
Thirty-Three Ways to Help with Reading by Raewyn Hickey

Thirty-Three Ways to Help with Reading

Supporting children who struggle with basic skills

Raewyn Hickey

Routledge
Taylor & Francis Group

LONDON AND NEW YORK

First published 2009
by Routledge
2 Park Square, Milton Park, Abingdon, Oxon OX14 4RN

Simultaneously published in the USA and Canada
by Routledge
270 Madison Avenue, New York, NY 10016

Routledge is an imprint of the Taylor & Francis Group, an informa business

Typeset in Bembo by Keystroke,
28 High Street, Tettenhall, Wolverhampton
Printed and bound in Great Britain by
Antony Rowe Ltd, Chippenham, Wiltshire

British Library Cataloguing in Publication Data
A catalogue record for this book is available from the British Library

Library of Congress Cataloging-in-Publication Data
Hickey, Raewyn.
  Thirty three ways to help with reading : supporting children who struggle
with basic skills / Raewyn Hickey.
    p. cm. — (Thirty three ways to help with)
  1. Reading—Remedial teaching. 2. Reading games. I. Title. II. Title: 33 ways
to help with reading.
  LB1050.5.H53 2008
  372.43—dc22   2008012952

ISBN 10: 0–415–44887–5
ISBN 13: 978–0–415–44887–1

Contents

Thirty-three ways to help . . . the series

This is a series of books to help teachers, teaching assistants and parents who want to help children to learn.

Most children at some stage or other in their school life come across something that they find difficult; a small minority of learners have difficulty in grasping the basic ideas presented in many lessons. Whichever the case, there is a need then for extra explanation and practice so that children can unravel any misconceptions, understand what is being taught and move on. Very often nowadays, this extra practice – or 'reinforcement' – is provided by teaching assistants (TAs) who are such a valuable resource in our schools.

Planning activities for TAs to use with children who need extra help can be challenging, however. There is little time for teachers to design 'mini-lessons' for TAs to use with individuals or small groups of children – and to talk them through the 'delivery' of such activities. This is exactly where the **thirty-three ways** series comes into play.

Teachers will be able to choose an appropriate activity for individuals or groups as part of their structured programme, or as a 'one-off' lesson for extra practice. The games and activities require no prior theoretical reading or knowledge and only a little preparation, so can be easily used by TAs or volunteer helpers in the classroom; teachers may also wish to share some activities with parents who want to know how to support their children at home. The activities use a multi-sensory approach to learning – visual, auditory and kinaesthetic; they have been designed for children aged 6–11 years, who need additional help with particular skills and concepts.

Teachers are constantly challenged to find ways to keep pupils motivated and to give them worthwhile 'catch-up' opportunities. But much of the photocopiable material available to teachers is too often 'busy work' that keeps children 'occupied' as opposed to learning. The books in this series provide a variety of adult-led activities that will keep children interested and take them forward in their learning. In this way, their confidence and self-esteem will grow as they experience success and have fun at the same time.

Series features

- Activities are practical (do not involve pencil-and-paper worksheets) and multi-sensory, to keep children motivated and enjoying learning.

- Activities do not require a lot of preparation and any materials required are readily available in classrooms.

- Activities are adult led, so children do not have the opportunity to keep repeating the same mistakes.

- Activities are grouped into different basic skill areas, so teachers can choose the activity best suited for a child's needs.

- Clear, concise reasons are set out for each activity.

- An extension activity is given, where appropriate, to challenge pupils and extend their learning.

Acknowledgements

I would like to thank Headteacher Mrs Avril Topping and the staff of Ravenbank Community Primary School Lymm for allowing me to trial the activities included in this book and for giving me such valuable feedback.

Introduction

As fluent readers, we know a lot about how language is organised: we understand about letter sounds, letters coming together to form words, words coming together to make phrases and sentences that create meaning for the reader. We know that written language is governed by rules. We can make predictions because some things are more likely to occur than others; for example, certain letter combinations are predictable and some words occur more frequently than others in predictable patterns. It seems logical then, that if children follow a sequence, they will learn to read.

There are some children, however, who cannot keep in step with a teaching sequence, no matter how effective the programme may be for the majority of learners. This book is designed to help those children who are not able to follow the usual path. They will need extra explanation, practice and encouragement.

- This book is divided into sections relating to the skill being taught. Each section begins with an introduction explaining why the skill has been included.

- The order of the sections is not intended to indicate a sequence for teaching. Instead, the sections are a helpful guide on where to find activities that will help your pupils discover a link they have missed.

- The tasks and games require children to be actively involved in their learning and to use logical, rhythmic, visual and kinaesthetic intelligences. Adult supervision is essential to move on or consolidate a child's learning.

● The games and activities have been carefully prepared so that anything needed can either be found in the school or quickly made using the photocopiable material provided.

Misconceptions

Many of the difficulties experienced by children learning to read are created, or exacerbated, by misconceptions – misunderstandings that confuse them and make it hard for them to move forward. It's important that everyone involved with teaching a child to read uses the same terminology and reinforces correct understanding.

For example:

phoneme	which means	one sound
grapheme	which means	a letter
digraph	which means	two letters making one phoneme

The National Literacy Strategy and commercially published reading programmes/schemes provide a glossary of terms nowadays – make sure that all teaching staff, assistants and helpers are familiar with these; parents too, will appreciate having this information. (There is also a glossary provided at the back of this book.)

Note: Throughout this book a child is referred to as 'he'. This is not to suggest a gender bias but is used merely as a way of improving fluency in the text.

A. Beginnings

Teachers use the terms 'letters' and 'words' frequently during reading and writing lessons. After a year or more at school, you would assume children have understood which is a word and which is a letter. Unfortunately this is not always the case, which is why the section on pointing (one-to-one correspondence) is included.

With the current emphasis on teaching letter sounds, you can expect children to be able to sound out two- and three-letter words. However, children need to remember several things when sounding out words – the sound relating to each letter, and how to blend each sound to make a word. It takes a lot of concentration, especially for beginner readers. For some children, sounding out letters has become the purpose of reading; they have been unable to spare enough attention to notice that some words are repeated more often than others. These children need to be taught a few essential frequently used words in order to free a little of their brain power to be able to pay attention to other important reading skills, such as making sense of the story and learning to read fluently.

Pointing to the words

The following activities are included to help those children who are not pointing to each word as they read, with the result that they miss out, or insert extra words.

Pointing is important because a beginner reader needs to know:

- for each spoken word there is an equivalent written word.

  If beginner readers have not realised this, they may also not know the difference between letters and words.

- to lift their finger off each word before pointing to the next one.

    Doing this shows you they know there are spaces between words and where the word begins and ends.

- how to point underneath each word.

    Readers will have more chance of noticing for themselves that the word they are saying matches the word they are pointing to if their fingers do not cover the words.

The adult should:

- never point for the child as they are reading.

    The message you are giving is *This is too difficult for you to do by yourself. You need an adult to help you.*

- encourage children to stop pointing as soon as they can always point accurately and they know around 35 high-frequency words.

    If the reading books are graded according to Book Bands, this stage would happen at about Band Three.

    Of course the children will need to point when they have made mistakes or the text becomes more difficult, but encourage them to take their finger away when the problem is solved.

- not ask older readers to point.

    Pointing at this stage often encourages children to read slowly.

    Pointing beyond the stage mentioned above decreases the children's chances of reading fluently and expressively.

Finding the words on the page

This is a way to learn to point by noticing the spaces between the words.

You may have noticed a child running his finger under a line of text. It may be that this child has not realised there are spaces between words that indicate the end of one word and the beginning of the next.

The child needs to see the spaces before you can ask him to point to each word as he reads.

Resources

- The child's reading book, or a big book that is well known.

Preparation

- Show the child the index fingers of your right and left hand, curling your other fingers and thumb into your palm.

- Tell the child these are your two pointing fingers.

- Ask him to show you his two pointing fingers.

- Tell the child he is going to 'catch' each word as he reads.

Activity

- Show him how to catch the words by reading the text on a page. As you say each word, put your left index finger at the beginning of the word and the index finger of your right hand at the end – in other words, in the spaces between the words.

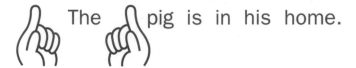 The pig is in his home.

- Ask the child to copy you, using his reading book, or the big book, encouraging him to 'catch' each word as he says it.

- At first the child will read very slowly as he gets used to the action. Ask him to read the same line of text three or four times, encouraging him to move his fingers into the spaces more and more quickly.

Extension

- Read two lines of print.

- Demonstrate how to 'catch' the words along one line and return to the beginning of the next line.

- Ask the child to copy your movements.

Pointing to the text

This is a way to learn how to point to text.

Resources

- Small triangle of paper for each child.

- A4 pieces of paper – one for each child.

- Objects such as plastic animals or cars.

Preparation

- Fold a triangle of paper into a cone small enough to fit securely onto the child's index finger.

- Make a cone for yourself as well.

> The cone is slightly harder for the child to manipulate than just a finger alone. It requires the child to think about getting the tip of the cone under each word.

Activity

- Put the collection of objects in front of the child. Ask him to choose one.

- Say: *Tell me about your . . .*

- Keep talking with the child for a minute or two (no more) about the object until you can agree on a short sentence about it.

- Write the sentence along the longest edge of the paper, keeping the space between the words extra wide. Some examples might be:

  My car can go fast.
  This is a cow.
  The lamb says 'Baa'.
  I like this car.

- Show the index finger of the hand you use to point with, and ask the child to do the same. Tell him this is his pointing finger.

- Tell him you are going to show him how to point to the words as he reads.

- Read the sentence to the child, pointing underneath each word with the cone on your finger.

- Ask the child to copy what you did.

- Ask him to repeat pointing, encouraging him to become quicker until he is pointing accurately and quickly, jumping his finger from one word to the next.

Extension: how print works on a page

- Write the child's sentence on two lines.

- Demonstrate by pointing along the first line as before and then returning to the beginning of the next line and pointing along to the end.

- Ask the child to copy your movements.

B. The alphabet

The activities in this section are included to help those children who have not been able to learn the letters of the alphabet as quickly as other learners.

Teaching letter names and letter sounds

Knowing the alphabet by letter name as well as by letter sound is important because:

- You need a language to talk about letters.

    A letter name is constant.

    Some letters change their sound according to where they come in a word. Look at words such as **gate** and **giant**; or **come** and **circle**. The sound of the **g** and **c** changes depending on what vowel comes next.

    Vowel sounds vary depending upon where the letter occurs in words.

- Teaching letter names avoids any confusion.

    The child is not confused when you say **c** or **k** but they can be if you use the sound.

    In words where the child cannot *hear* all the letters it is more logical to be able to say 'You cannot hear it, but this word is spelt with the letter **a** as well' rather than giving the sound.

    Two vowels together make only one sound – a long vowel sound, which is usually the letter name of the first vowel.

The adult should:

- consistently talk to children about what they can *hear* using letter sounds, and talk about what they can *write* or *see* using letter names.

Children have no difficulty in learning letter names and sounds at the same time when both are used consistently in the right context.

Confusing letters

In every infant classroom there will be children who confuse the letters **b** and **d**, **p** and **q** and sometimes **b** and **p**. Frequently these confusions are not problems with reading, but with writing. When children begin to write, they usually form letters haphazardly; forming **b** the same way as a **6** for example or beginning both **b** and **d** with a downward stroke and then not knowing which side of the 'stick' to write the 'round bit' on.

Once handwriting habits are established, they are very hard to change despite every effort made by teachers.

Some ideas for solving confusions

a) Before the child knows all the letters of the alphabet.

- Always teach letters which are likely to cause confusions in different weeks.

- Wait until one letter is firmly established before introducing the similar letter.

- When the child can correctly name and sound one of the letters during one lesson, and another on a separate occasion, then the two letters can be used together in the same lessons. (See 'Recognising letters by shape' and 'Letter sort' activities.)

b)   Handwriting practice

- For young children, make sentences like the examples below. Write them onto cards for the children to see.

- Each sentence can be sung to a tune such as *Cows in the Kitchen* or *Skip to my Lou*. For example:

Baby bears bouncing b b b (letter sound)
Baby bears bouncing b b b
Baby bears bouncing b b b
And this is how we write it.

● At the end of the last line, ask the child to form the letter in the air; with a finger on the floor/table/partner's back; on a white-board; with paint; in the sand. Instead of paint, you can use water and a clean paintbrush and write letters on the concrete outside.

B b

Baby bears bouncing

D d

Ducks are diving

● For older children, to illustrate that *d* has the circle on the left and *b* has the circle on the right use rhymes such as the following. Try doing actions to the first verse and writing in the air for the second.

Which Way Now?

b is for bowling,
ball and bat.
Bat to the right of you,
And that is that.

d is for ducklings
diving and dip.
Ducks dive to the left,
Now use the tip.

Start with a down stroke
Then back up,
Round to the right
And join it up.

Start with the letter c
And up to the top,
Bring your pencil down again
So the 'd' won't flop.

An alphabet book

This is a way to start learning new letters when a child can name fewer than ten.

Resources

- Felt tip pens or coloured pencils.

- A book with 26 pages made from unlined paper to make an alphabet book with the child – one letter for each page.

- Paste.

- Pictures or drawings of items which have the known letter as the initial letter.

- Pictures or drawing of items which have the new letter as the initial letter.

Before beginning the activity

- Write the capital and lower-case letters that the child knows into the book.

- Show the child the alphabet book and ask him to find the pages which have a letter he knows. Ask him to say the letter names.

- Choose the letters one at a time and show the child the pictures that start with that letter.

- Ask the child to choose the picture he thinks he would remember best to go with the letter.

● Paste one picture into the book to go with the letter.

It may be the child has a different word that he associates more closely with the letter. In that case, draw it very quickly, or ask the child to draw it.

Activity

● Say: *Today we are going to learn a new letter. It is* (name the letter) *and it goes on this page* (write the capital and lower case into the alphabet book). *It makes the sound* (make the sound as clearly as possible without putting an 'ah' sound at the end).

● Spread out the pictures to go with the new letter and go through them with the child.

● Say: *Which picture is the best one to help you remember this letter?* Paste or draw in the book the picture the child chooses for that letter.

● Go through the book asking the child the name and sound of other known letters that have been written in.

NB: It is important to teach only one letter in each session.

Extension

● Use the alphabet book for the recognition of the upper-case letters.

● Cover the lower-case letter on the page before you show the child the name and sound of the upper-case letter.

Sounds practice

These are ways of practising initial sound recognition and matching the sound to the letter.

Resources

- Plastic letters.

- Timer.

Activity

- Place some plastic letters on the table – three or four might be enough in the early stages, progress to more letters as the child improves. Ask the child to find the letter *b*. When he has identified the correct letter shape, ask him to look around the room for something beginning with that letter. Encourage him to keep saying the sound while he thinks – help him if necessary: *'b, b, b, box. That's right, box begins with a b doesn't it?* Vary the task by asking the child to think of:

  - animals

  - people's names

  - items of clothing

  - items in a picture

- Hide plastic letters around the room behind/under objects beginning with the appropriate sound – set the child the task of finding

2, 3 or 4 letters within a certain time: *'I've hidden three plastic letters under things beginning with '**b**' – see if you can find them before the sand runs through the timer – remember to say the word beginning with '**b**' when you find the letter.*

● Praise the child for correct answers. When he offers an incorrect word, say something like: *Mmmm, let's think about that for a moment. We're trying to think of a word beginning with 'p' – you say it – 'p'. So bear isn't quite right is it? Bear begins with a 'b'. P, p, p . . . what about 'pig'?*

This can be repeated frequently in short bursts, while standing in the lunch queue, waiting for the lesson to begin, travelling on the bus or in the car.

Extension

Put picture cards on the table and ask the child to pull out all the things beginning with a certain sound – if there are two or three children, they can compete to see who gets the most.

Two letters, one sound (1)

This is a way to learn the sounds of the digraphs *sh*, *th*, *ch* and *wh*.

Resources

● One photocopy of the sound cards.

Preparation

● Photocopy a set of the sound cards on page 15. Leave the cards black and white so that the child does not associate colour with the pictures.

● Cut out each picture.

● Write a sentence on the back of each card as shown below:

Baby is going to sleep 'sh'

A tyre going flat goes 'th'

The tug boat goes 'ch'

The wind goes 'wh'

Activity

● Teach the child the sound each picture represents by holding up the card close to your mouth and reading the phrase and sound on the back of each card.

● When the child can look at the picture and make the correct sound, move on to the next activity.

Sound cards

sh	th
wh	ch

Two letters, one sound (2)

This is a way to learn the sounds of the digraphs *sh*, *th*, *ch* and *wh*.

Resources

- Two photocopies of the sound cards on page 15, one for yourself and one for the child.

Preparation

- Cut out the cards.

- Leave the cards black and white so that the child does not associate colour with the pictures.

Activity

As soon as the child can associate the picture with the sound:

- Choose two sound pictures from the set, that is, the child has only two pictures in front of him.

> For this activity, the child does not need to know what each word means. He only needs to hear the sound.

- Say: *I am going to read out some words. As I say each one, I want you to listen to the sound at the beginning of the word and point to the picture that says that sound.*

- Read words from the lists below that correspond to the sound cards in front of the child.

Words with digraph at the beginning

sh	th	ch	wh
shout	the	chin	while
shoe	that	chat	when
shop	thin	chop	what
ship	think	Charlie	whether
shadow	thunder	chatter	

Extension

- Give the child three cards.

- Give the child four cards,

- Choose words from the list below with the letters at the end of the words.

For the extension activity, the child does not need to know what each word means. He only needs to hear the sound.

Words with digraph at the end

sh	th	ch
mash	with	pinch
fish	path	branch
bush	earth	catch
wash		

● Choose words with the letters in the middle of the word.

Words with digraph in the middle

sh	th	ch	wh
ashes	brother	attachment	nowhere
fashion	something	parchment	meanwhile
cushion	nothing	coachhouse	somewhat
worship	northern	searchlight	
midshipman	without		

● Choose words from all three lists.

● When the child can associate the picture with the sound in words, move on to the next activity.

Two letters, one sound (3)

This is a way to learn the sounds and letters of the digraphs *sh, th, ch* and *wh*.

Resources

- Photocopies of the sound cards.

- Photocopies of the letter cards.

Preparation

- Photocopy a set of sound and letter cards for the child and a set for yourself.

Activity

- Say: *We are going to learn the letters that make the sounds we have been learning*. Spread out the set of sound cards and match the letter cards to each one.

- Hold up the picture of the mother and sleeping baby and the **sh** card.

- Teach the child the following song to help him remember the letters that make the sound.

- Sing the following jingle to the tune of *Happy Birthday to You*.

When we see 's' (use letter name) *and 'h'* (use letter name),
They make the sound 'shhhh'.

When 's' (use letter name) *and 'h'* (use letter name) *are together,*
They make the sound 'shhh'.

> Using the letter names when teaching digraphs (two letters that form one sound) is very important because the individual letter sounds do not blend to make the sound you are teaching.

- Repeat the song, substituting the different letters according the sound being taught.

- Ask the child to match his sound cards and letter cards.

Extension

- As soon as the child can match the letter and sound cards consistently, repeat Activity 6 but use the letter cards instead of the sound cards.

Recognising letters by shape

This is a way to start recognising letters by shape, when a child can name fewer than five.

In this activity you are asking the child to notice something unique about the shape of the letters. You are not asking him to give the sound the letter makes or to name the letter.

Resources

- Multiple numbers of three or four different magnetic or plastic letters. For example:

    If one of the letters is **h**, find as many **h**'s as you can.

    Choose different colours for each letter if you can, that is, try to find **h** in different colours, otherwise the child may do the activity sorting by colour, rather than the letter.

- Three or four small hoops (maths set rings are ideal), large tiles or carpet squares.

Preparation

- Choose three (or four) letters, making sure you have several of each one. Put them to one side.

- Choose letters that are distinctly different. For example, **c t w p** have observable differences whereas

    a c   **d b**   **g p q**   **m n**   **v w**   **i j l t**   are similar.

- Place the three (or four) hoops or squares in front of the child.

- Place two of each of the letters the right way up below the hoops or squares.

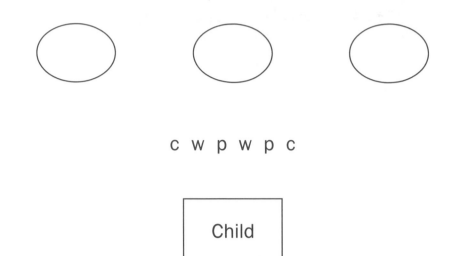

c w p w p c

Child

Before beginning the activity

- Point to one of the letters.

- Say: *Look at this letter. Can you find a letter that is the same shape? Can you find a letter that is a different shape?*

- Ask the child to tell you what is different.

- Answers (using the example above) could include:

    This one has a stick going down (p) and this one is round at the bottom (w).

    This one is like a circle (c) and this one is like a circle with a stick (p).

    This one has a stick with a cross (t) and this one has three small sticks (w).

If the child cannot see any differences, help by pointing out something unique in the letter and ask if another letter has the same thing. Then ask the child what he can see that makes the other letter look different.

Activity

- Place all the letters you have chosen in front of the child.

- Say: *We are going to sort these letters into these hoops. Can you put all the same shaped letters into this hoop?*

- When the child has sorted one set, say: *Put all the same shaped letters into this hoop.*

- When the child has sorted the next set, ask him to sort the next one (and the last one if there are four sets).

- Gather up the letters and put them in front of the child again. Say: *Can you sort them all out this time? How fast can you sort them?*

Extension

- Choose letters that are very similar in shape.

Letter sort

This is a way to start learning new letters when a child can name fewer than ten.

As this is a reading activity, not a writing one, you are asking the child to name a letter (see introduction to this section).

Resources

- Multiple numbers of three magnetic or plastic letters that the child can recognise and the new letter you want the child to learn. For example:

    If one of the letters is **h**, find as many **h**'s as you can.

    If you can, choose different colours for each letter, that is, try to find **h** in different colours, otherwise the child may do the activity using the colour, rather than the letter.

- Four small hoops (maths set rings are ideal), large tiles or carpet squares.

Preparation

- Choose three letters the child knows and the new letter, making sure you have several of each one.

- Choose letters that are distinctly different For example, **c t w p** have observable differences whereas

a c   d b   g p q   m n   v w   i j l t are similar.

- Place the four hoops or squares in front of the child.

- Place the letters the right way up below the hoops or squares.

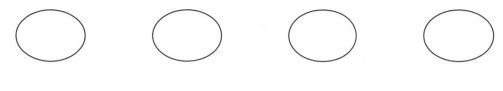

c t w p w p c t

w p c p t p t c w

Child

Before beginning the activity

- Slide the new letter away from the others.

- Say: *This letter is called . . .* (name the letter). *Can you find another . . .* (name the letter).

- Point to the letter and ask: *What is this letter called?*

Activity

- Place all the letters you have chosen in front of the child.

- Say: *We are going to sort these letters into these hoops. Put all the* (name the letter) *into this hoop.*

- When the child has sorted one set, repeat until the child has sorted each of the letters into the hoops.

- Gather up the letters and put them in front of the child again.

- Say: *I want to sort them again, but this time I'm not going to tell you the letters because I think you can sort them by yourself. Show me how quickly you can sort them.*

- When the child has sorted the letters into the hoops, ask him to name the set of letters in each hoop.

● Ask the child to sort the letters again, encouraging him to work as fast as he can.

Extension

● Choose letters that the child has learned very recently as well as one new letter.

Upper- and lower-case letters

This is a way to start learning both the upper- and lower-case letters.

Resources

- Photocopy of the *To and Fro Letters* game board on page 31 enlarged to A3 size.

- Dice.

- One counter for each player.

Preparation

- Choose which letters are going to be used in the game, and write the lower-case letter into the squares marked *x* and the corresponding upper-case letters into the squares marked *y*.

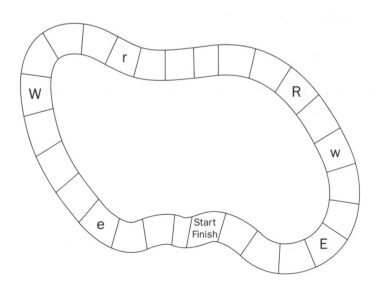

27

Rules

- A player throws the dice and moves his counter the corresponding number of squares.

- If his counter lands on a square with a letter written in it, he moves to the other square with the same letter.

- This means the player could move forwards or backwards on the board.

- The winner is the first person to reach the Finish square.

Activity

- Say: *Today we are going to play a game called the 'To and Fro Letters' game. First, put your counter on the start line.*

- Ask the child to throw the dice and move the corresponding number of squares.

- Then take your turn.

- If either the child's or your counter lands on a square with a letter, say: *When you land on a letter you have to move your counter to another square that has the same letter. What letter is that? Can you see another* (name the letter)?

- Continue the game until one person reaches the Finish square.

Alternatives

- This game can also be used to teach letters and sounds.

- Choose which letters are going to be used in the game.

- Write the letters into the squares marked *x* and a corresponding picture with the initial sound into the squares marked *y*.

Extension

- Choose pairs of pictures that have the same initial sound.

- Paste one of the pair in a square marked *x* and the other in a *y* square.

To and Fro Letters Game Board

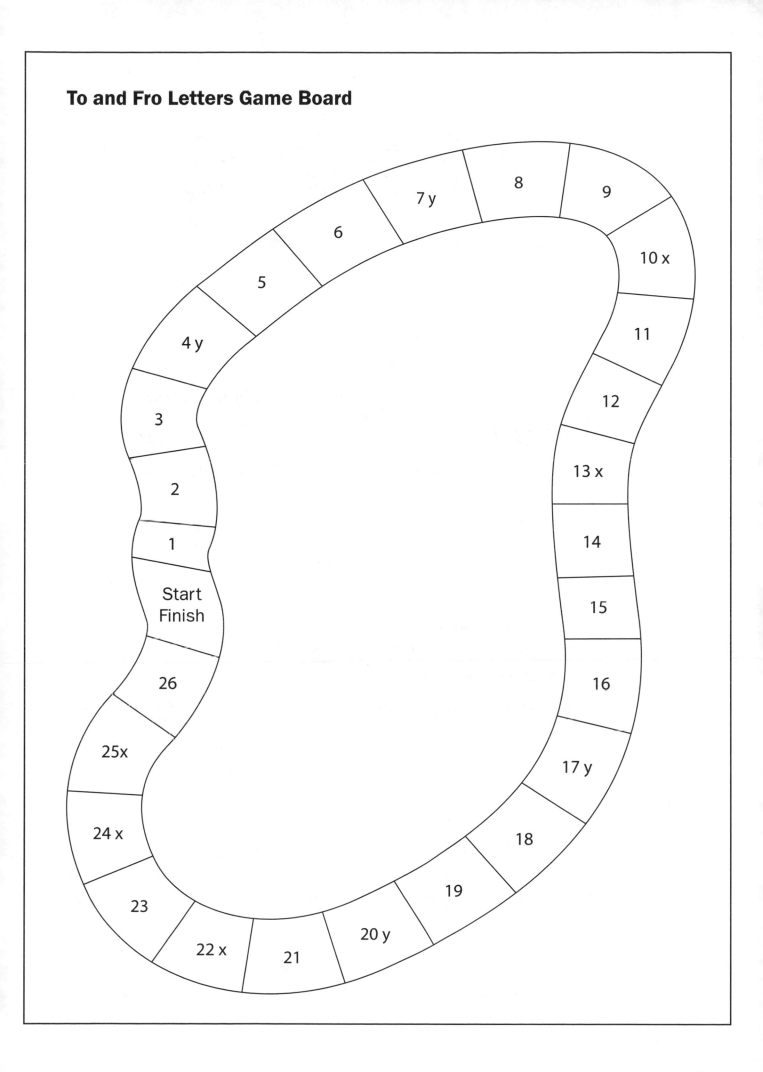

C. Learning high-frequency words

The following activities are included to help those children who cannot quickly recall a few frequently used words.

Knowing some words is important because a beginner reader needs to:

- have a sense of security.

    Imagine yourself as an early reader confronted with a page of words.

    Imagine the words flowing across the page like a river.

    ⌗ą§ əĥβ͞ă« #★±¥⌗ µ±★#áfş ⌗ą§ #★±

    Knowing those little words that are always used in text is like having secure stepping stones as you negotiate your way across, for example, whenever you see µ± you know it is always going to say *to*.

- feel successful as a reader

    As soon as beginner readers can point accurately, they can begin to notice the individual words. Knowing some frequently used words lets beginner readers correct their own mistakes as they read — a vital step towards becoming an independent reader.

    Children who can notice and correct a mistake as they read are seeing themselves as readers — they don't always need someone to help them. They are building their self-esteem.

- use less energy tackling every word on the page.

    Having to work out each and every word takes a lot of time and energy. The more words beginner readers can recall instantly, the more they can concentrate on the meaning of the story and on working out the harder words.

The adult should:

- not send a list of words home for children to learn to recognise.

    It is all too easy to give children the wrong idea about reading, that is, that it is all about memorising words.

    The new word the children are learning should be taken from real text and put back into text so children do not see the learning as an isolated exercise.

- choose which words to teach from the children's guided reading book.

    There are a number of lists of high-frequency words; there is one in the *National Literacy Strategy* of words to learn in Reception.

    The words taught can be chosen in any order.

    You do not need to teach all the words on the list.

    Children need to be able to instantly recall about 15 of the most frequently used words before they can successfully tackle anything other than the simplest, earliest texts. (Book Band 1.)

- teach only one word at a time.

    Children who find it hard to remember need to build up a bank of words slowly to begin with, or they will forget the ones they learned the day before or last week.

    Make sure the children can recall all the previously learned words before teaching another one.

- teach a new word that has different letters or looks very different to the word taught the lesson before.

    Children would become easily confused if *my* was introduced one lesson and *me* the next or *in, is* and *it* taught one after the other.

    You could teach words such as *on* and *to* on subsequent days as the shape they make is very different.

Wordmaker

This is a way to learn a new frequently used word.

Resources

- The child's guided reading book – the book should have a frequently used word in a sentence on every page.

- Plastic or magnetic letters to make that word.

- If you are working with a group you need enough of the same letters for each child.

Preparation

- Make the word from the letters.

- Place the letters for the word in a pile ready for the activity.

- Give the child a copy of his guided reading book.

Before beginning the activity

- Ask the child to open his book at any page and point to the word . . . (name the chosen word).

- Ask the child what the word says, that is, the one he is pointing at.

- Ask the child to turn to another page and point to the (same) word.

- Ask the child what the word says, that is, the one he is pointing at.

- Repeat once or twice more.

Activity

- Ask the child to keep his book open so he can see the new word.

- Give the child the pile of magnetic letters.

- Say: *Here are the letters to make . . .* (the word). *Put them down and make the word.*

- Ask the child to check his book to see if he has put the letters in the correct order.

- Say: *What is the word you have made?*

- Ask the child to close his reading book.

- Say: *Pick up the letters and jumble them up in your hands. Put them down and make . . .* (the chosen word) *again.*

- If the child has arranged the letters in the wrong order, do not correct it at this point.

- Say: *Open your reading book and find the word. Is yours the same?*

- Say: *What is the word you have made?*

- Repeat the task of closing the book, jumbling the letters, remaking the word and checking with the reading book two or three more times.

> Remember to ask the child what the word is that they have made. Sometimes a child can become so focused on the physical activity involved, they forget what the word actually is.

Extension

- Choose enough letters to make three or four words that the child can recognise. For example:

    h i e e s m t

- Give the letters to the child in a jumbled pile.

- Ask him to make as many words as he can from the letters.

- In the above example the child would probably make *the is me*.

- Ask the child to read the words he has made.

- Pick up the letters and add the letters for the new word.

- Say: *I have put in some more letters. What words can you make now?*

- Ask the child to read the words he has made.

More high-frequency words

This is a way to learn a new high-frequency word as well as practising previously learned words.

Resources

- Small cards or pieces of paper.

- Felt tip pen.

Preparation

- Write a different known word on each piece of paper. You will need to make a set of words for each child if you have a group of children. Keep a blank piece for the new word. For example:

up	to	my	the	

Activity

- Give the child the group of words:

- Say: *Spread the words out so you can see them.*

- Say: *Find . . .* (name one of the words). (Ask the child to point to the word.)

- *Find . . .* (name another word).

- Repeat once more.

- Write the new word on the blank piece of paper and show it to the child.

- Say: *This new word is . . .* (name the word).

- Ask him the read the new word.

- Say: *Pick up all the words and jumble them up.* (Including the new word.) *Now spread the words out again so you can see them.*

- Say: *Find . . .* (name one of the words). (Ask the child to point to the word. Include the new word as you repeat the task several times.)

- Say: *Read the word you are pointing to.*

Extension: word bingo

This game can be played when the child knows up to seven or eight words.

- Make a list of the words the child knows.

- Divide a card or paper into four or six squares.

- Write a word in each square. If you are going to play this game with a group of children, and need to use some words again, change the order of the words on each card. For example:

go	me
is	to

to	me
on	go

- Give the child four (or six) counters.

- Read a word from the list. If the child has the word on his card, he covers it with a counter.

- If a group is playing, the first child to cover all his words is the winner.

Crocodile, crocodile

This is a way to practise high-frequency words.

This game is adapted from an old playground game.

Resources

- Three or four whiteboards/cards for each child.

Preparation

- Write a different known word on each of the whiteboards.

- Place the whiteboards word side down, in vertical lines and in the same order. Leave a space between each one big enough for the child to stand in.

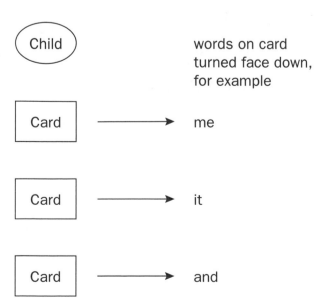

Before beginning the activity

● Say: *We are going to play a game called Crocodile, crocodile. Each of the whiteboards in front of you is a stepping stone to get you across the river. If you can read the words on the boards, you can step up behind the next one. First we need to practise what to say to the crocodile in the river. You say 'Crocodile, crocodile, may we cross the shining river?'*

● Ask the child to repeat the chant.

● Say: *After you say that, I say 'Yes, if you can read the word on the board.'*

● Practise the chant and the answer.

Activity

● Ask the child to stand behind the line of cards.

● Say with the child: *'Crocodile, crocodile, may we cross the shining river?'*

● Say: *'Yes, if you can read the word on the board.'*

● Say: *Turn over the first board and read the word.*

● If the child reads the word correctly, he steps behind the next board.

● If he reads the word incorrectly, he stays where he is.

● On the next turn, the child will have a second attempt at the word and move on.

Playing the game with a group

● Make a set of word cards for each child.

● Place each line in a different order face down on the floor. For example:

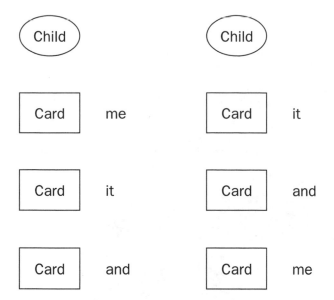

- Ask each child in turn to read the word in front of them. The Crocodile chart on page 40 can be used to record progress.

Extension

- Play the game with more than four words.

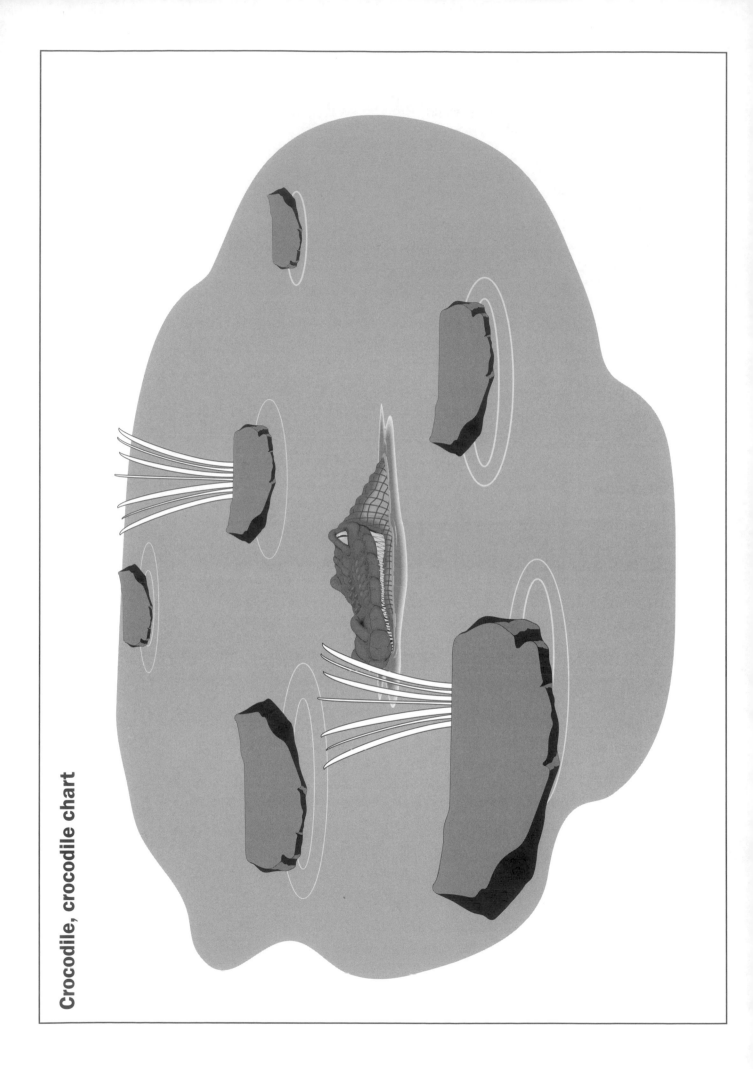

Bean bag bingo

This is a way of recognising and remembering words that are used frequently in text.

Resources

- Five or six known high-frequency words written on paper or card.

- Small bean bag or something soft to throw.

Preparation

- Write one known high-frequency word on each card. (You could use whiteboards but the words may become blurred after a few throws of the beanbag.)

- Place a marker to indicate where the children should stand to throw the bean bag.

- Put the cards randomly on the floor at different distances from the marker.

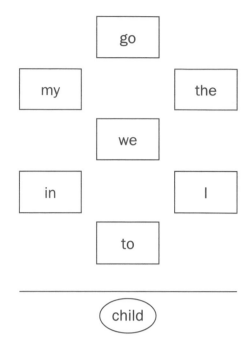

Activity

- Ask the child to throw the bean bag to land on a word, or as close as possible to a card.

- Ask him to read the word the bean bag landed on or near. If he can't read the word, ask another child to help, or tell him the word yourself and ask him to repeat it before his next go.

- If you want to add an element of competition, you could give the child a point for every word he can read correctly. The next time the child plays the game he can try to improve his score.

- Change the words on the cards as the child learns more frequently used words.

- Keep a star chart or record sheet to show the child how many words he can read correctly.

Extension

- Play the game as above, but turn the word cards face down so the child cannot aim for the word or words he knows.

- Ask him to turn over the card and read the word the bean bag landed on or near.

D. Making links: phonics

Systematic, direct teaching of synthetic phonics is the first strategy taught to all children learning to read. From the beginning of schooling, children are taught a small group of letter sounds very rapidly, and are shown how these letter sounds can be sounded and blended together in order to work out a word. When appropriate, particular groups of letters are taught, and the children blend them in order to pronounce new words. Digraphs (where one sound is represented by two letters, for example, **sh**, **th**, **ch**, **oa**, **ai**) are explicitly taught, but the sounds two consonants make together (such as **st**, **sp**, **br**, **fr**, once referred to as consonant blends) are not, as they can be read by blending.

The following activities are included to help children to blend letter sounds together, to notice groups of letters that combine to make sounds that don't correspond to the letters, and to recognise regularly used word endings.

Blending letter sounds

It is important for a beginner reader to be able to blend letter sounds together:

- When decoding new words.

- When the word contains a digraph.

    Children must be able to notice when words contain vowel or consonant digraphs.

    Children must know two vowels together make one sound, for example, **ea**, **ai**, **oa**, **ou**.

The adult should:

- Pronounce the letter sounds as 'cleanly' as possible. That means you need to be very careful how you say the sounds.

rrr	not	**ruh**
l	not	**luh**
mmm	not	**muh**
ch	not	**chuh**

- For the children who have found blending a difficult skill, hearing sounds pronounced with **uh** at the end and copying that sound, then makes blending letters together even more difficult.

- You may need to ask a colleague to listen to you say the sounds if you are unsure. It is often difficult to hear your own pronunciation.

Verb endings

Some children, when reading, will see the verb endings **ing** and **ed** and expect each letter to have a separate sound. Teaching the children how these endings sound through singing and actions is a way of helping them to remember.

You can make up any actions to go with the songs. One way would be to teach the children to use their whole bodies to make the letters (as closely as possible).

Bean bag blending

This is a way to practise blending sounds together to read an unfamiliar word.

Resources

- One bean bag.

- Whiteboards or card.

- Felt tip pen.

Preparation

- Write the following words onto small whiteboards or card, one word on each.

    most, **camp**, **small**, **bend**, **tram**, **still**, **yelp**

- Place a marker on the floor to indicate where the child should stand to throw the bean bag.

- Put the cards randomly on the floor, each at a different distant from the marker.

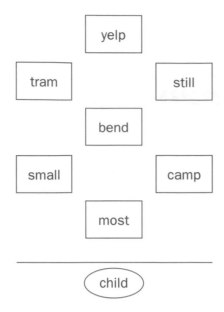

- Ask the child to throw the bean bag so that it lands on a word, or lands as close to it as possible.

- Ask him to read the word the bean bag landed on or the closest one to it, by sounding out each letter quickly and joining the sounds together.

- Encourage the child to sound the letters without pausing between each sound.

- If you want to add an element of competition, you could give the child a point for every word he can read correctly: double points can be given for the word he finds most challenging. When playing the game on other days, the child can see if he can improve his score.

Extension

- Choose words with five or more letters.

N.B. Each letter of the word must make an individual sound so words that have two vowels or two consonants together that make one sound should not be included. For example words with **sh**, **ch**, **th** or **wh** should not be included unless you know the child has learnt these sounds.

Words with **ai**, **ay**, **ow**, **ea**, etc., should also not be used unless you know that children are familiar with vowel digraphs (two vowels making one sound).

Ladder sounds

This is a way to learn how to blend sounds together to read unfamiliar words.

Resources

- Photocopy of *Ladder Sounds* game board on page 51 enlarged to A3 size.

- Photocopy of *Ladder Sounds* cards on page 52.

- Dice.

- Counters – one for each player.

Preparation

- Cut the *Ladder Sounds* words into individual cards and place face down in a pack near the game.

Rules of the game

- A player throws the dice and moves his counter the corresponding number of squares.

- If his counter lands on a square with a ladder in it, he turns over a card and blends the sounds to read the word.

- If he reads the word correctly he moves up the ladder.

- The winner is the first person to reach 30.

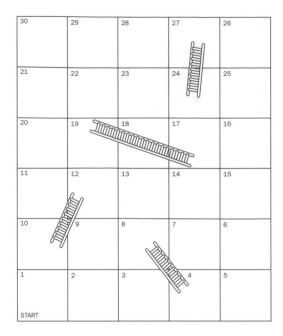

Activity

- Say: *Today we are going to play a game called 'Ladder Sounds'. First, put your counter in the first square to start.*

- Ask the child to throw the dice and move the corresponding number of squares. Then take your turn.

- If either the child's or your counter lands on a square with a ladder, say: *When you land on a square with a ladder in, you turn over the top card in the pile and read the word by blending the sounds together. If you can read the word you can move your counter up the ladder.*

- Continue the game until one person reaches the final square.

Extension

- Make new cards with longer words.

- You must be able to hear every letter in the word. For example, you could not have words with silent letters.

- Only use words which have consonant digraphs, that is, words with **th**, **ch**, **sh**, or **wh**, when you know the children have learned them.

Ladder Sounds

30	29	28	27	26
21	22	23	24	25
20	19	18	17	16
11	12	13	14	15
10	9	8	7	6
1 START	2	3	4	5

Ladder Sounds cards

flap	began	rental
sent	wind	elf
cleft	text	stub
pedal	film	plum
trumpet	bled	strap

Snakes and Ladders Sounds

This is a way to practise reading words that contain vowel digraphs.

Children should not be introduced to this game until they have an understanding of vowel digraphs – two vowels making one sound.

Resources

- Photocopy of *Snakes and Ladders Sounds* on page 53 enlarged to A3 size.

- Photocopy of *Snakes and Ladders Sounds* cards on page 54.

- Dice.

- Counters – one for each player.

Preparation

- Cut the *Snakes and Ladders Sounds* words into individual cards and place face down in a pile near the game.

Rules of the game

- A player throws the dice and moves his counter the corresponding number of squares. If his counter lands on a square with a ladder in it, he turns over a card and reads the word.

- If he reads the new word correctly, he moves up the ladder.

- If a player lands on a snake's head, he slides down to the tail.

- The winner is the first person to reach 30.

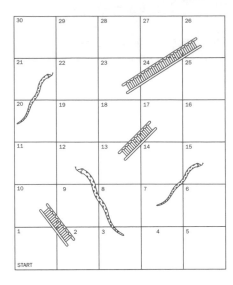

Activity

- Say: *We are going to play 'Snakes and Ladders' with words. If you land on a square with a ladder, you climb up. If you land on a snake's head, you slide down.* The child throws the dice and moves the appropriate number of squares.

- When a counter lands on a ladder square, say: *When you land on a square with a ladder in it, you turn over the top card in the pile and read the word by saying the sounds and blending them together. If you can read the word you can move your counter up the ladder.*

- If the child is able to read the new word, he can climb the ladder to a new square. If not he stays in the square.

- If a player lands on a snake's head, he slides down the snake to its tail.

Extension

- Play the game with other words. Use words with two vowels together at the beginning or in the middle of the word and also words which end with a split digraph; for example, **east**, **team**, **plate**. Choose longer words; for example, **hesitate**, **treatment**.

Snakes and Ladders Sounds

30	29	28	27	26
21	22	23	24	25
20	19	18	17	16
11	12	13	14	15
10	9	8	7	6
1 START	2	3	4	5

Snakes and Ladders Sounds cards

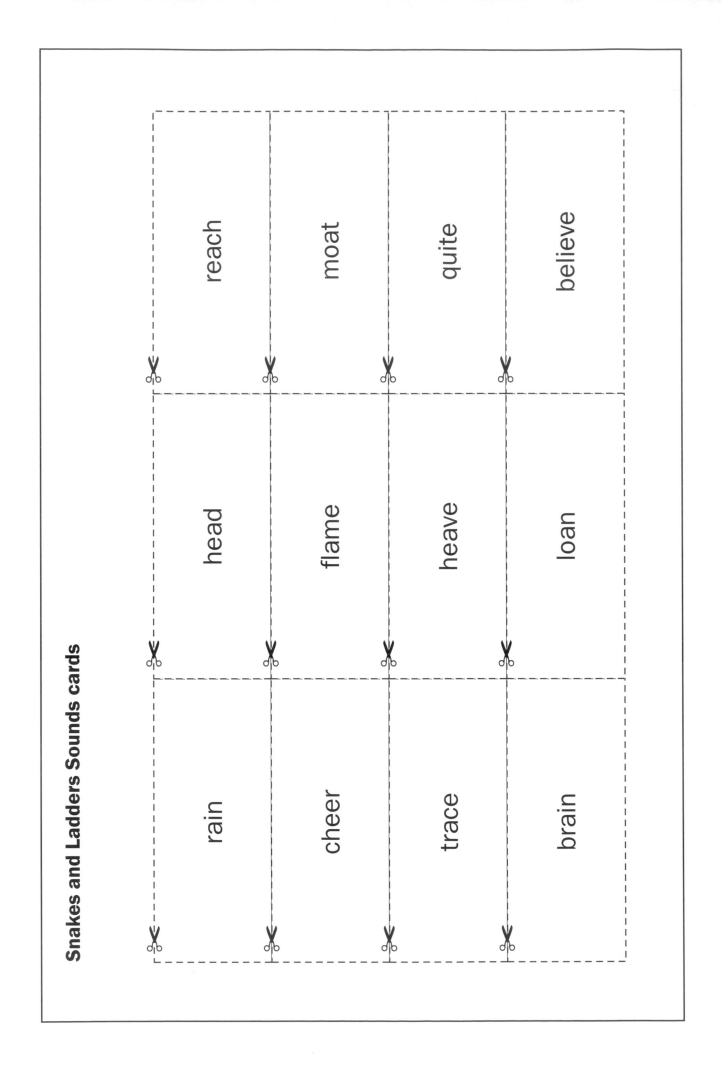

rain	head	reach
cheer	flame	moat
trace	heave	quite
brain	loan	believe

54

Tricky words

This is a way to learn some of the letter combinations that have different pronunciations.

Resources

- Photocopy of tricky words cards on page 58.

- Four maths set rings or circles.

- Small drum.

Preparation

- Cut the tricky words into individual cards.

- Spread the cards face up on the table.

- Place the set rings close to the cards.

Activity

- Say: *For this activity I want you to look at the word cards and decide which cards belong together. When you have found some, put them in a circle, then look for another group.*

- Repeat until the cards have been sorted into the four circles.

Set 1	Set 2	Set 3	Set 4
brought	conversation	colour	tension
nought	mention	valour	mansion
fought	stationary	favourite	occasion
thought	creation	labour	evasion
sought	position	saviour	erosion

- Say: *Tell me why the cards in this hoop* (indicate set) *belong together.* Repeat with all the sets

- The child should have sorted the words into the four groups above, giving reason such as:

  These all have **ought**.

  These all have **tion**.

  These all have **our**.

  These all have **sion**.

- If the child has misplaced a few of the cards or gives a different answer, say: *Take the cards out of the hoops. Now I am going to put some cards together and I want you to tell me why I think they go together.*

- Make one of the sets

- If the child has difficulty, ask him to look at the words and find the letters that are the same in each word.

- Put two words into a hoop and ask the child to find two more words that would belong.

- When the sets are sorted correctly and the child can name the groups of letters in each set, say: *We are going to learn how these letters sound together.*

- Say the sounds for the child, pointing to each group '*ort*', '*shun*' etc.

- Spell the letter groups and say the sound. Ask the child to join in.

- Turn it into a chant and give the child the drum to tap the rhythm, for example:

o   **u**   **ght**   **is**   **ort**   **ort**   **ort**

tap   wait   tap   wait   three short taps   tap   tap   tap   tap

t   **i**   **on**   **s**   **i**   **on**

tap   wait   tap   wait   two short taps   tap   wait   tap   wait   two short taps

both   **say**   **shun**

tap   wait   tap   wait   tap

Extension

- Ask the child to choose a book and together look for words that have the letter combinations the child has been learning. You could also photocopy a page from a book and ask the child to use a high-lighter pen to mark the words with the letter combinations learned.

Tricky words cards

brought	conversation	colour	tension
nought	mention	valour	mansion
fought	stationary	favourite	occasion
thought	creation	labour	evasion
sought	position	saviour	erosion

Comparing

This is a way to learn letter patterns in tricky words.

This game is adapted from the game musical chairs.

> Before attempting this game, children should have some knowledge of letter combinations. For an introduction to letter combinations, try the activity 'Tricky words' on page 55.

Resources

- Card/paper or whiteboards $\times$ 8.

- Pen.

- Music on tape or CD or drum or tambourine.

Preparation

- Choose four words from list A and four from list B.

- Write one word on each card.

- Spread the cards in a large circle on the floor, placing them so they are the right way up from the outside of the circle.

List A		List B	
Words with three or more letters to make one sound		Words with digraphs	
brought	remember	brief	rescue
conversation	never	branch	reprove
bright	soluble	bait	proclaim
colour	cripple	pith	latitude
thought		lunch	
straight		avenue	
valour		daisy	
mention		weary	
flight		opposite	
nought		clench	
stationary		flounce	
mansion		delete	
favourite		crime	
tension		austere	

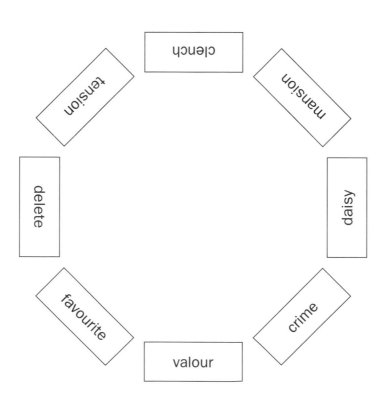

- Prepare either a CD or tape for music, or have a drum or tambourine to hand.

60

Activity

- Say: *This game is a bit like musical chairs. I am going to play some music* (beat the drum) *while you walk around the outside of the letters. When the music* (drum) *stops, stay standing behind the word you have reached.*

- Ask the child to begin walking and play the music for a few seconds. When the music stops, say: *Look at the word on the floor in front of you. Is it a word with a digraph, or is it a word with three or more letters that make one sound?*

- Award a point if the child is correct. The child is not expected to read the word.

- Say: *Which two letters make the sound?* or *Which letters make the sound?*

- Award another point if the child can correctly identify the letters.

- Take the card out of the circle and repeat the sequence.

Extension

- In this game the child is not expected to be able to read the words but if he can, award him another point.

- When the game is ended, ask the child to collect the cards which have words containing a digraph, and ask him to sort those words into ones which have a vowel digraph and ones where the digraph is made from two consonants.

Pattern and rhyme

This is a way to learn the sounds groups of letters make together.

Before using this activity, make sure the child can hear rhyme and continue a rhyming pattern. If the child is unable to hear rhyming words, or to say a word which rhymes with another, use one of the activities from the letter patterns section starting on page 73.

Resources

- Photocopy of the nonsense rhymes on page 67.

- Photocopy of the word endings cards on page 67.

- Highlighter pen.

Preparation

- Cut the word endings from page 67 into individual cards.

- If you choose to play the game on another day, make a copy of the words list for each child.

Before beginning the activity

- Show the child the copy of the nonsense poem.

- Say: *I'm going to read you this nonsense poem. As I read it I want you to listen to the sounds of the words. At the end, I'm going to ask you what sounds you heard at the ends of the words.*

- Let the child see the nonsense verse as you read it quite slowly.

- You want the child to hear the rhyming syllables at the ends of the words. If the child has not heard the syllables that sound the same, repeat the verse, stressing the rhyming syllables at the ends of words.

Listen now,
Teach**er**, tail**or**, sold**ier**, sail**or**,
Atten**tion**, atten**tion**, the train's at the sta**tion**.
It is n**ight** and there is no l**ight**.
This is awful, horr**ible**, terr**ible**.
We can't find M**able**.
She's under the t**able**.

- Repeat the nonsense verse with actions to fit in with each line. For example:

First line	pointing to imaginary people
Second line	standing to attention
Third line	peering into the dark.

- When the child has heard the rhymes, say: *Which letters are the same in the words on each line? Take the highlighter pen and highlight the letters that are the same. Look at the letters you have highlighted. Think about the verse. What sound do the highlighted letters make?*

- Go through the highlighted sounds with the child.

- Say: *Which syllable makes the **able** sound. The **ible** sound? The **ite** sound? The **shun** sound? The **a** sound?*

Activity

- Spread the word ending cards on the table for the child to see.

- Say: *We are going to play a game using the sounds we have been looking at in the poem. I'm going to close my eyes and I want you to choose one of the cards. Turn it upside down. Gather up the rest of the cards and put them in a pile so I can't see them.*

- Say: *Now I have to work out which card you have. I am going to ask you questions. You are only allowed to answer 'yes' or 'no'. I am not allowed to ask which line of the poem the letters are in, or to say the sound.*

- The questions to ask include:

   Does the sound begin with (give a letter name)?

   Is the sound in the word . . . (give a word)?

   Is the sound in a word that rhymes with . . . (one of the rhyming words)?

- When you have found the right ending, say: *The card makes an* (name the sound) *sound.*

- Repeat the game, this time letting the child ask the questions.

- Play the game again but this time using nonsense rhyme 2.

Extension

- Play the game again on another day. Choose *one* of the word lists on page 67. Photocopy and cut out a copy for each player.

- Ask the child to read the words in the list before you play the game.

- Ask the child to choose one of the word ending cards as before, then choose a word from the word list that has the same ending as the word ending card.

- Tell him not to tell you his word, or word ending card.

- The player asking the questions is now trying to work out the word the second player has chosen from the word list. For this game you are not allowed to say the sound or ask if the sound is in a particular word from the list, but you can give a rhyming word. The two questions to ask are:

   Does the sound begin with (give a letter name)?

   Is the sound in a word that rhymes with . . . (a word that rhymes with one in the list)?

- Demonstrate the game first by asking the questions and finding the child's word. When it is the child's turn, encourage him to use both questions.

Word endings

er/or	tion	ight
ible	able	

Word list

A	B	C
incredible	breakable	doctor
fight	mention	edible
fable	printer	slight
fraction	sensible	laughable
splinter	right	detention

Nonsense rhyme 1

Listen now, teacher, tailor, soldier sailor,

Attention, attention, the train's at the station.

It is night and there is no light.

This is awful, horrible, terrible.

We can't find Mable.

She's under the table.

Nonsense rhyme 2

I thought you said you brought the cake.

No, I didn't. Remember?

We fought and I said

Kevin ought to bring the cake.

Just be delightful, grateful and thankful

And thank Kevin nicely and politely for the cake.

Follow the sound

This is a way to learn some of the sounds in words where the letters combine to make a different sound.

Resources

- Photocopy of *Which Ones Match?* cards on page 68 or a list of the words.

- Four hoops for the player to stand in.

- Four small whiteboards or four squares of paper.

Preparation

- Spread the hoops out giving as much space as possible between them.

- Write the following on the whiteboards or paper, one letter group on each.

     igh   tion   our   ough

Before beginning the activity

- Show the child the cards with the letter patterns. Say the sounds and ask the child to repeat them.

- Ask the child to point to each letter pattern and say the sounds by himself.

- Read a word from the *Which Ones Match?* list and ask the child to point to the letter pattern he heard in the word.

- When the child can remember the sounds, place one whiteboard or paper inside each hoop.

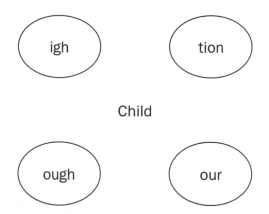

Child

Activity

- Ask the child to stand in the middle of the space with the hoops spread around him.

- Say: *I am going to read a word from my list. Listen carefully. The sounds that we have been practising could come in the middle or at the end of the word. Run and stand in the hoop when you think you know the letter pattern in the word.*

- Award a point for each sound the child gets right.

Extension

- Ask the child to choose a hoop to stand in.

- Ask him to say a word that contains that sound.

Which Ones Match? cards

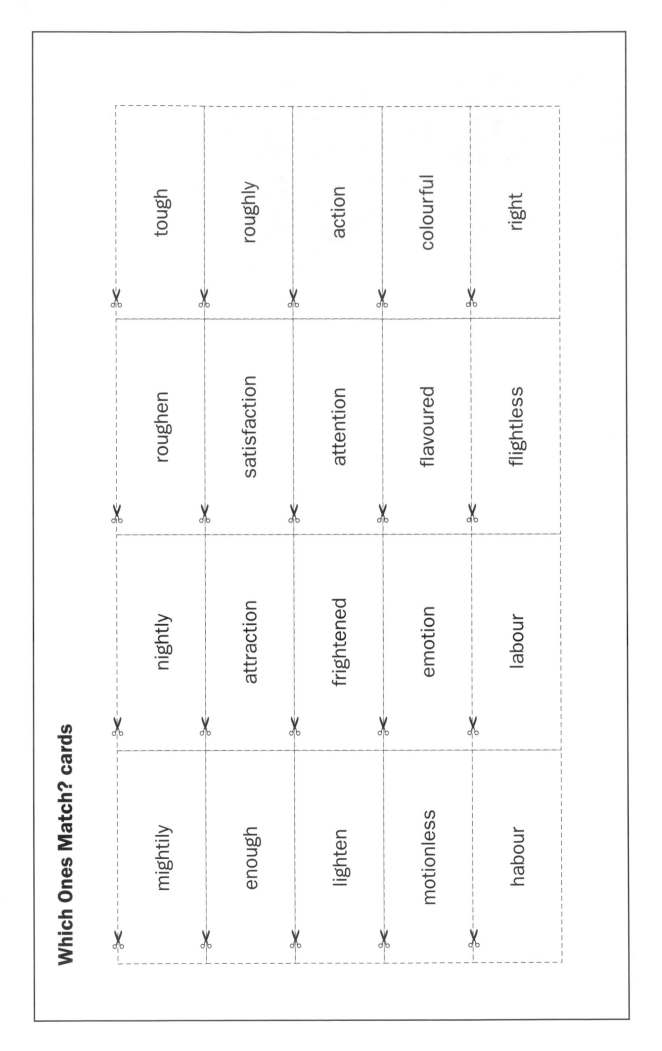

mightily	nightly	roughen	tough
enough	attraction	satisfaction	roughly
lighten	frightened	attention	action
motionless	emotion	flavoured	colourful
habour	labour	flightless	right

Which Ones Match?

This is a way to remember some letter patterns where the letters represent one sound.

The following two games are variations of *Snap!* and *Consequences*.

Resources

- Photocopy of *Which Ones Match?* cards on page 68.

Preparation

- Cut *Which Ones Match?* cards into individual word cards.

- Shuffle the cards out of the order in which they appear on the photocopy.

Rules of game 1

- Place the cards word side down in four rows on the table.

- The players take turns to turn over two cards.

- If the cards contain the same letter pattern, the player keeps the pair of cards.

- The winner is the player who has the most pairs of cards when all the cards have been picked up from the rows.

Activity

- Say: *We are going to play a game you may have played before. But these cards are different. When it is your turn, you turn over two cards. If the words on the cards have the same letter pattern, you keep them and you can have another turn. If the two words don't have the same letter pattern, you turn them back over and it's the next person's turn.*

Extension

- The player can only keep the pair if he is able to sound the letter pattern.

Rules of game 2

- Shuffle the word cards and deal them evenly between two players.

- The first player takes the top card from their pile and puts it into the middle.

- The second player takes the top card from his pile and puts it onto the card in the middle.

- The players continue to take turns putting cards down.

- If a player notices that two cards in a row have the same letter pattern, he says 'Snap!' and can pick up all the cards from the middle.

- The game ends when one player has all the cards.

Activity

- Say: *We are going to play 'Snap!' with word cards. We are going to take turns to put a card down. If you spot that your card has the same letter pattern as the one underneath, you say 'Snap!' and you can pick up all the cards in the pile.*

Extension

- The player can only pick up all the cards if he can sound the letter pattern.

E. Letter patterns

Rhyme

The following activities are included to help those children who need practice in hearing the same sounds in different words.

If a child is experiencing difficulty in doing this, it is always worth considering whether he is hearing well enough. Many young children have a recurring condition known as 'glue ear' that can impair hearing significantly, so be aware of this possibility and consult with parents if you have concerns.

Knowing about rhyme and words that rhyme helps children to:

- understand the pattern of syllables as they hear them.

- recognise rhyming strings.

- recognise syllable patterns in new words.

- read words with the same letter pattern.

Alliteration

Hearing patterns in words helps children to:

- develop their vocabulary.

- develop their writing skills.

Making rhymes

This is a way of hearing and composing rhymes.

Resources

- Photocopy of the *Ladder Sounds* board on page 49.

- Dice.

- Counters – one for each player.

- Word list.

Preparation

- If you have already played *Ladder Sounds* with the child, use the same board for this game but you do not need the *Ladder Sounds* cards.

- Write the following words in a list. Choose either the easier list A or the harder list B depending on the child's reading ability. This list is given to the child to read later in the game.

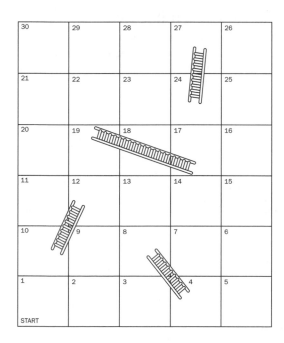

List A	List B
spot	shake
shut	match
chat	hive
thin	cling
beg	shout
slim	roam
shop	sneak
bent	theme
tent	cave
plum	meadow

Rules of the game

- A player throws the dice and moves his counter the corresponding number of squares.

- If his counter lands on a square with a ladder in it, read two lines from one of the rhymes on pages 74–75 to him, stopping before the last word.

- If the child can tell you a rhyming word to finish the line, he can move up the ladder.

- The winner is the first person to reach 30.

Activity

- Say: *Today we're going to play a game called 'Making Rhymes'. Put your counter in the first square to start.*

- Ask the child to throw the dice and move the corresponding number of squares.

- If the child's counter lands on a square with a ladder, say: *You've landed in a square with a ladder in it, so now I am going to read you part of a rhyme and you have to think of a word to finish it.*

- Choose either the easier playground skipping rhymes or the harder rap on page 75, depending on the maturity of the child.

- Read two lines and stop before the last word. If the child can say a suitable rhyming word, he can move his counter to the top of the ladder.

- Then take your turn.

- If you land on a ladder, ask the child to choose a word from the list for you to say a rhyming word.

- Continue the game until one person reaches the final square.

Extension

- Choose pairs of rhyming words from one of the rhymes and ask the child to give one, two or three more rhyming words.

Playtime skipping rhymes

When I was three I scraped my knee,
When I was four I could reach the door,
When I was five I saw a bee hive,
When I was six I could do high kicks
When I was seven my sister was eleven,
When I was eight I dropped Mum's plate.

Teddy bear, teddy bear, dressed in blue,
Can you do what I tell you to?
Teddy bear, teddy bear, turn around.

Teddy bear, teddy bear, touch the ground.
Teddy bear, teddy bear, do the splits.
Teddy bear, teddy bear, give a high kick.
Teddy bear, teddy bear, go upstairs.
Teddy bear, teddy bear, say your prayers.
Teddy bear, teddy bear, turn out the light.
Teddy bear, teddy bear, say good night.

Playtime rap

Miss was reading poetry and tapping with her pen,
When suddenly she stopped and she said 'Now then,
Listen here children', and she went snap! snap!
'Snap your fingers, to the playtime rap.'

She picked up a pencil, and she moved her feet,
'Copy me children, to the playtime beat.
Grab your skipping rope, grab that ball,
Clap to the rhythm as we rap down the hall.'

We rapped across the classroom and out the door,
We clapped down the hallway, we stamped on the floor,
We snapped our fingers and we tapped our toes,
Just like they do it in the video shows.

Dinner ladies rap

Do you want baked beans my love?
Harry, please don't push and shove.

Would you like a fork my dear?
Edna come and help me here.

Stacey what's that, on the floor?
Don't you dare go out that door.

Fred, I know there's food you hate
You still can't put it on Tom's plate.

I can hear the playground bell,
Thank heaven for that. Today's been hell.

Rhyming throw

This is a way of making rhymes.

Resources

- Five small whiteboards or squares of paper.

- Pen.

- A small bean bag or something soft to throw.

Preparation

- Write the numbers 1 to 5 on the whiteboards or paper – one number on each board.

- Write a word from the following list underneath each number. Be careful to write the easiest rhyming words on the boards with the higher numbers.

leaf	self
groan	glad
leant	clench
clean	hair
tomorrow	sunk

- Place a marker to indicate where the child should stand to throw the bean bag.

- Put the boards randomly on the floor, with each at a different distance from the marker.

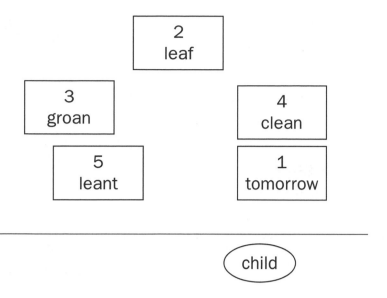

- Ask the child to throw the bean bag so that it lands on a number, or to land as close to it as possible.

- Ask him to read the word closest to the bean bag, and then think of the number of rhyming words written on the board. For example, the bean bag lands on

| 5 |
| leant |

the child has to say five words rhyming with *leant* (e.g. bent, sent, dent, meant, tent).

- If you want to add an element of competition, you could give the child a point for every board he completes correctly. Remember, the words need to rhyme, but do not have to be spelt the same way.

Extension

- Only write the numbers on the boards.

- After the child has thrown the bean bag, choose one of the following rhymes.

- Read the two lines, leaving out the last word. The child has to think of the rhyming word to end the line as well as the extra rhyming words depending on the number on the board. For example if the child lands on 4, he gives the rhyme at the end of the line and adds three more rhyming words.

  Wee Willie Winky ran up the stair
  Wee Willie Winky said a prayer

Humpty Dumpty fell to the ground
Humpty Dumpty was never found

Mary had a small blue kite
She thought it was a lovely sight

Little Boy Blue get out of the corn
Your feet are all muddy and your coat is torn

Pussy cat, Pussy cat, won't you come here?
I'm much too sleepy, but I am quite near.

To and Fro Rhymes

This is a way of practising hearing rhymes.

Resources

- Photocopy of the *To and Fro* game board on page 29 enlarged to A3 size.

- Dice.

- Counters – one for each player.

Preparation

- Choose pairs of words from the list below to use in the game. Write one of the words in an *x* square and the other in a *y* square on the board.

Rhyming pairs		Rhyming pairs	
hop	top	shop	flop
tin	pin	chin	thin
pen	men	dent	went
sand	hand	plan	than
lip	rip	trip	ship
let	wet	much	such
sat	at	when	then
sun	fun	jelly	smelly

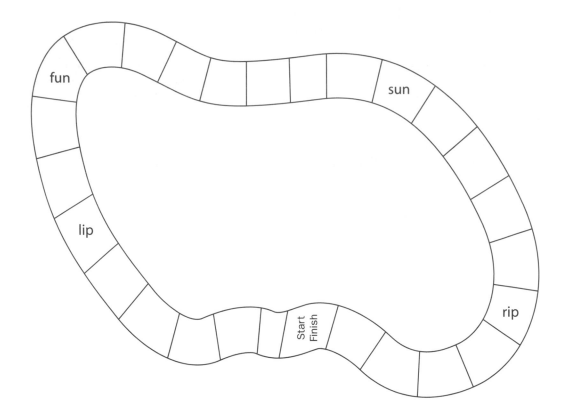

Rules

- A player throws the dice and moves his counter the corresponding number of squares.

- If his counter lands on a square with a word written in it, he moves to the square with a corresponding rhyming word.

- This means the player could move forwards or backwards on the board.

- The winner is the first person to reach the Finish square

Activity

- Say: *Today we are going to play a game called 'To and Fro Rhymes'. First, put your counter on the start line.*

- Ask the child to throw the dice and move the corresponding number of squares.

- Then take your turn.

- If either the child's or your counter lands on a square with a word, say: *When you land on a word, you have to move your counter to another square that has a rhyming word.*

Extension

- Choose words that rhyme but have different spellings

Rhyming pairs

been	cream
many	penny
climb	time
they	today
soar	poor
foot	put
break	flake
torn	yawn

- Ask the child to give two more words with the same initial sound, or first two sounds.

- Ask the child to give two more words to make an alliterative phrase. For example:

    Benny has been batting.

    Brian broke Brenda's bat.

F. Making sense of text

Reading text

At the Foundation Stage and into Year 1, children learn the sounds that letters make and how to blend letter sounds together to make words. Alongside that skill runs the knowledge that we always read texts for meaning. An older reader may blend sounds to work out an unfamiliar word, but actually mispronounce it: even so, he or she may still have an understanding of what the word means because of the supporting, surrounding text. This is of great help with working out tricky words, for example, 'We went to London and took a boat trip on the river *Thames*'. The word 'Thames' is difficult to get to by using phonics alone – but a child who has heard the name of the river running through London will use his own knowledge and the supporting text to get to the word.

Reading for meaning

- Supports the reader's attempts at blending sounds – texts should always make sense, so a child will notice his own mistakes when a sentence doesn't make sense.

- Means the reader is depending on prior knowledge about how stories work/his knowledge of the world/storybook language.

Research and anecdotal evidence shows that introducing the text to a child before he attempts to read it, makes the task easier; this is especially true for reluctant readers or children who find reading difficult.

Reading non-fiction text

Traditionally, most children have been taught to read from fiction texts. This is changing as schools buy new reading books that include a range of fiction and non-fiction titles. Non-fiction texts require readers to read not only for meaning, but also for information.

Reading for information and understanding will require readers to:

- re-read sections for text for better understanding.

- scan text searching for a key word or phrase.

- skim read to gain a quick overview of what the text is about.

- find headings and subheadings which relate to the information they need.

- summarise text orally or in writing to be sure they understand information.

Sentence strips

This is a way of practising reading, reinforcing familiar words and recognising new words out of context.

Resources

- The child's reading book.

- Strips of paper wide enough to write on.

- Pen.

- Scissors.

Preparation

- Ask the child to choose a sentence from his reading book, or work together to compose a sentence.

Activity

- Write the sentence on a strip of paper or card and cut it up into single words, asking the child to read it as you make each cut. Always cut the punctuation into its own card. For some children, it may be easier to start by simply cutting the sentence into two parts to begin with, progressing as soon as possible to individual words.

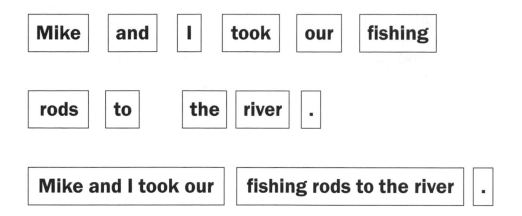

- Mix up the cards on the table but make sure you leave them the right way round.

- Ask the child to put them in the right order to make the sentence.

- As he does so, ask him to read the words as he goes along.

- Do not correct any mistakes at this stage.

- If the child can't find the next word, ask him to re-read the part of the sentence he has already completed to help him remember the word that comes next.

- When the child has completed the sentence, ask him to read it through, pointing to each word.

- If the child has made a mistake in the word order, give him time to notice it for himself.

- Tell him there is a word out of place.

- Ask him if he can read the sentence again looking carefully at the beginning letters.

- You can then mix up the cards again, and ask the child to remake the sentence.

- You might like to put the words into an envelope, write the sentence on the front as a reminder, for the child to take home and practise with parents or to keep safe for reviewing the following day.

- This will make a collection of sentences for the child to revisit and practise on a regular basis.

Extension

- Choose and write two sentences from the child's reading book to sort in the same way. Make sure you cut the punctuation into its own separate card.

Self-checking

This is a way of teaching how to combine visual cues (phonics) and meaning cues to check whether the text has been read correctly.

Resources

- Whiteboard or paper to write on.

- Small cards and blu-tak™ or sticky notes.

- Story book, that is, a book *you* will *read to* the child. If working with a group choose a big book.

Preparation

- Cover a few individual words in the text so the child cannot see them. Two or three sticky notes trimmed and stuck together are usually thick enough to hide the writing. Do not choose words too close together because the child needs to get an understanding of the story. For example:

'Who ate the last chocolate biscuit?' demanded Sam.

Sam turned round and ⬚ at his brother and sister who were sitting on the floor watching television.

'It's not fair,' cried Sam. 'I didn't get one.'

'Never mind,' said his brother, not taking his eyes off the ⬚, 'You can have an extra helping of carrots at dinner to make up for it.'

- Read the story up to the covered word and stop.

- Say: *What word could be under there?*

- Write the suggestions the child makes on a whiteboard or paper.

- Uncover the first letter of the word.

- Say: *Do any of the words you thought of start with this letter?*

- If not, say: *What word would make sense here and start with . . . (letter)?*

- You may need to read the last sentence again.

Alternatively

- Instead of uncovering the initial letter, uncover the first two of three letters if it has consonants at the beginning.

- Say: *This word starts with these letters. What sounds do they make together? What word would make sense here and start with . . .* (the sounds).

- Or, uncover the last letters if it is a verb ending with **ing** or **ed**.

Extension

- Choose longer words with two or more syllables.

- Uncover the final syllable.

- Or, show the middle syllable by moving the paper to one end, and covering the beginning with your finger.

Silly stories

This is a way of reading text for meaning and enjoyment.

Resources

- A book at the child's reading level that the child has not read.

- Sticky notes.

- Sheet of paper.

- Pen or pencil.

Preparation

- Choose a number of pages from the book that contain at least five adjectives *or* adverbs.

- Cut rectangles from the sticky note and cover five adjectives *or* adverbs.

Before beginning the activity

- Say: *Before you begin reading, I want you to write five adjectives (adverbs).*

- If the child does not know what an adjective is, say: *Adjectives are the interesting describing words that tell you more about the person or thing in the story. For instance, how would you describe this pen (pencil)? If the story was set in a forest, what words could you use to describe it?*

- Adjectives include words for:

  colour (red, blue)

  size (long, squat, round, tubby)

  emotions (happy, bewildered, joyful).

  If the child does not know what an adverb is, say: *Adverbs tell you **how** something is done or happens. They often end in **ly** but not always.*

- Adverbs describe the verb. They include words to describe how something:

  moved

  stood

  spoke or made a noise.

- Help the child write five adjectives or adverbs.

Activity

- Ask the child to open the book ready to begin reading.

- Say: *We are going to make this into a funny story. I have covered up five adjectives (adverbs). When you come to a word that is covered up, read the first word on our list instead. At the next covered up word, you will read the second word on the list and so on.*

- Tell the child a little bit about the text before he begins reading. For example, say: *This is a story about . . . The character/characters is/are . . . He/She/They are about to . . .*

- Ask the child to read the story, substituting the words in order from the list for the words you have covered up.

- Enjoy with the child the peculiar choices of adjectives/adverbs that are now in the story and how it makes the story sound.

Extension

- Cover up to ten adjectives or adverbs in the text.

- The substituted words are (hopefully) inappropriate in the context. Ask the child what adjective or adverb would have been a better choice.

Character tree

This is a way to understand the relationships between characters in a story and why they act the way they do.

Resources

- A reading book at the child's reading level that has not been read – the book should be a story about a family or a school story.

- A3 paper.

- Pen.

Preparation

- Read the story quickly so that you know the relationships between the characters.

- Before beginning the activity, introduce the book to the child by telling him who the main character is and where the story takes place.

Activity

- Ask the child to read the story.

- When the child has finished reading, give him the paper and pen.

- Say: *We're going to think how the characters in this book know each other. Start by writing the name of the person the story is about, in the middle of the page. Now who else is in the story? Write the name somewhere else on the page and draw an arrow to the name in the middle. How do they know*

. . . (the main character)? *Along the arrow, write a word to describe how these two people know each other.* For example: friend, mother, grand-father, etc.

- Go through all the characters in the story in the same way.

- Choose an incident from the story where a family member is interacting with the main character.

- Say: *If you were . . . (the main character) would you . . . have done/said/behaved like that? Why do you think . . . did/said that in this story?*

- Choose an incident from the story where a friend is interacting with the main character.

- Say: *Do you know people who do/say things like that? Why did . . . do that in this story? Why has the author made the characters behave like this?*

- Talk with the child about where authors get their ideas from and how they make their characters behave like real people.

- Talk about relationships and why mother/father/sibling/friend behave or react in certain ways.

Extension

- Draw a family tree in the conventional manner, using either another story or the child's family.

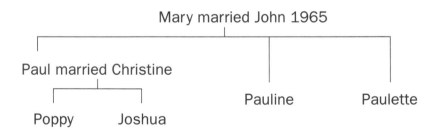

Finding the facts

This is a way of reading a non-fiction text for information.

Resources

- A non-fiction book at the child's reading level that the child has not read, which has headings and subheadings.

- Strips of paper.

- Pen.

Preparation

- Choose a section of the text that is not too long to be read in one session.

- Read the headings/subheadings and consider which ones could be turned into questions. Choose question beginnings from the following:

Where (or When) is . . . ?	Where (or When) can . . . ?	Where (or When) can . . . ?
Why is . . . ?	Why can . . . ?	Why did . . . ?
How is . . . ?	How can . . . ?	How did . . . ?
What is . . . ?	What can . . . ?	What did . . . ?
Which is . . . ?	Which can . . . ?	Which did . . . ?
Who is . . . ?	Who can . . . ?	Who did . . . ?

- Write the question beginnings you have chosen in a list to be used during the activity. For example:

  When is . . . ?

  How did . . . ?

  Why did . . . ?

- Before beginning the activity introduce the text to the child by explaining briefly what the text is about.

Activity

- Ask the child to find the headings and subheadings in the text.

- Ask him to find the first heading/subheading.

- Show him the short list of question beginnings you have prepared.

- Say: *How could you change the heading/subheading into a question? Look at this list of question words and decide which one would be the best to use to make this heading/subheading into a question.*

- Write the question on a strip of paper and lay it across the text so it covers the original heading/subheading.

- Repeat the same exercise with the other headings/subheadings in the piece of text you have chosen.

- Once the headings/subheadings have been changed into questions, say: *Go back to the first question. Read the question and then read the text underneath. As you read, I want you to think about the question and see if you can find the answer as you read the text.*

- Repeat the same process with each question.

Extension

- Show the child how to make notes:

- When the child has read the text and found the answer to the question, ask him to give the answer in three to five words.

- Ask him to write the answer down – tell the child this is called 'making notes'.

Questioning skills

This is a way of using questions to read fiction for meaning.

Resources

- A fiction book at the child's reading level that the child has not read.

Preparation

- Quickly read the book/chapter/pages of text the child will read during the lesson.

- Use some of the following question to prepare five or six questions to ask during and after the reading.

- Decide which questions are appropriate to ask during the reading and which should be asked at the end.

These types of questions develop the child's *reasoning* skills as he thinks about the text:

- Why do you think x behaved like that (did that)?

- What would you have done?

- If x had done/said/gone . . . how would the story have ended?

These types of questions develop the child's *creative thinking* skills as he talks about the text:

- Who was in the wrong/did the wrong thing?

- What is this character thinking at this moment/in this picture?

- Where is *y* while *x* is . . .

- Do you see this hill/house/wall in the picture? Who could be walking along behind it?

- If . . . came just then what would . . . say/do?

- If . . . was looking out the window/over the wall/through the fence what would he/she see?

These types of questions develop the child's skills to *enquire* about the text:

- What do you think will happen when . . . ?

- What if . . . ?

- What else could have . . . ?

- What would happen next if . . . ?

- Before beginning the activity, introduce the book to the child by telling him who the main character is and where the story takes place.

Activity

- Ask the child to begin reading.

- Ask your prepared questions at the appropriate sections during the reading, and at the end.

- Talk with the child about:

    how he reached his answer

    why he thinks that

    what bit in the story made him think that way.

- If the child finds a question difficult, direct him to re-read the sentence/paragraph which will help him.

Extension

- You pretend to be a character in the story.

- Ask the child to think of questions beginning with *What if . . . ?* *Why did . . . ? When . . . ?* he would like to ask the character. You answer as if you were the character.

- The child takes on the role of a character. You ask the questions which the child answers in role.

What's he like?

This is a way to reflect on characters and understand their actions.

Resources

- Photocopies of the character cards on page 101.

- Child's reading book.

Preparation

- Cut out character pictures to make into cards.

- Before beginning, introduce the book to the child by telling him who the main character is and where the story takes place.

Activity

- Ask the child to read the text.

- At the end of the reading, place the character cards face up on the table.

- Say: *These cards represent the way that characters in books behave, and the type of people they are.*

- Go through each picture asking the child what characteristics they think the pictures represent. For example:

  What kinds/types of people like to climb mountains?

  How do foxes behave? What do people think of them?

What kind/type of person would the thought bubble be for?

What sort of person would you need to be to be a fireman?

The characteristics you are looking for are things such as:

- adventurous
- likes to take risks
- doesn't think about dangers
- rushes into things

- thinks problems through
- calm
- doesn't get upset easily

- sneaky
- clever
- likes to trick people
- has clever ideas

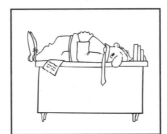

- lazy
- doesn't care
- doesn't want to get involved
- cowardly

- courageous
- helpful
- caring

- practical
- knows how to do things
- can solve problems

- Ask the child to think about the story and one of the characters in particular.

- Say: *Choose a card to show what sort of person X is in the story.*

- When the child has chosen the card, say: *Can you find the bit in the story that tells you he/she is like that?*

- Repeat the exercise with another character.

Extension

- Choose one incident from the story.

- Ask the child to choose a picture to represent how the character behaved during it.

- Say: *Is there another place in the story where . . .* (the character) *behaved differently? Which card best describes him/her for this part of the story?*

Character cards

Crosswords

Crosswords are a favourite activity with children when they are pitched at the appropriate level. Making simple crosswords yourself ensures that individual children are presented with the right amount of challenge and can achieve success.

For developing readers, using words from their current reading books can be very supportive and provides opportunities for them to practise reading text and using letter cues (phonics).

Resources

- The child's reading book.

- Squared graph paper.

- Pen or pencil.

Preparation

- Choose between 6 and 12 words from the text. You need words that have varying numbers of letters with one letter in common between pairs of words.

- Write one word across the middle of the squared paper. Choose another word to go down from it, putting the letter common to both at the start, middle or end of the second word.

```
h a i r y
a
v
i
n
g
```

- Add another word across and another one down from that.

```
          m
h a i r y  o
a          u
v e n o m o u s
i          t
n          a
g          c
           h
           e
```

- Use the letters already there to join on more words either down or across, remembering to keep at least one square between words.

- Number the squares where the words begin.

- Write clues for the words across and words down in separate lists.

- At the end of each clue, write the number of letters in the word.

- Write the page numbers of the text for the child to begin. For example:

You will find the answers between pages 2 and 6 of (title of current reading book)

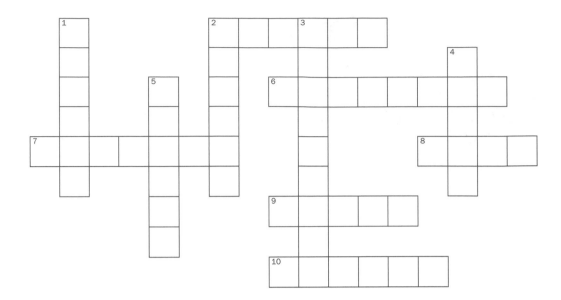

Across

2. Cookie swiped with his _____ paw. 6
6. His eyes were _____ . 8
7. Name of baby zebra _____ . 7
8. The saliva began to _____ from Cookie's jaws. 4
9. His mouth was getting _____ . 5
10. 'We will _____ him overnight,' said the vet. 9

Down

1. Animal in the next cage. 6
2. Cookie didn't want the vet _____ a thermometer at him. 6
3. The smell of fear was _____ to an angry bear. 9
4. Cookie was very _____ . 5
5. It dripped from his jaws. 6

Using crosswords

● Show the child the crossword and tell him which pages he needs to read to find the answers.

● Ask the child to read the first clue. Ask him to read the pages indicated to find the answer and write the name putting one letter in each box.

● Continue to help until the child understands how to fill in a crossword. As the child progresses, make the crosswords more challenging by using more clues and making the clues harder – perhaps using synonyms for example.

Glossary

Adjective An adjective is a word that describes a person, place or object. Adjectives come before the person or object they are describing as in:

> Conrad helped the old man

or after linking verbs such as be, look, get, seem, as in:

> This shoe seems bigger
> The dinner looks delicious

Adverb An adverb gives additional meaning to a verb, an adjective or another adverb.

> The man walked slowly (verb + adverb)
> The boy's coat was extremely dirty (adverb + adjective)
> The man walked really slowly (adverb + adverb)

An adverb can move around in a sentence.

> *Quietly*, the man walked into the house.
> The man *quietly* walked into the house.
> The man walked into the house *quietly.*

Blend Blending is the process of running the sounds of letters together to make a syllable or word.

Consonant Consonants are all the letters of the alphabet excluding a, e, i, o u.

Digraph Two letters represent one sound (sh, ch, etc.)

High-frequency words These are the small two, three and four letter words used most often in sentences; for example: **the, is, to, get, I, go, look, said.**

Initial letter The first letter in a word.

Lower case Letters written as small letters (a, b, c) not capitals (A, B, C).

Meaning cues The clues children can get when they are reading, from the pictures and the developing story line.

Split digraph Two vowels which represent one sound with a consonant between (the second vowel being e); for example: **tape, like, stripe.**

Syllable When a word is tapped out as a rhythm, each beat is a syllable.

Upper case The name given to the letters when they are written as capitals (A, B, C).

Visual cues The clues in the text that the child can see as he is reading, that is, the letters and the sounds the letters make.

Vowel The letters of the alphabet – a, e, i, o, u.

Vowel digraphs Two vowels which represent one sound (ea, oa, ou, etc.).